GIRL I CAN'T HAVE

WHERE IT ENDS, IT BEGINS

NITESH REDDY

BookLeaf Publishing
India | USA | UK

Presentation by *BookLeaf Publishing*

Web: www.bookleafpub.com
E-mail: info@bookleafpub.com

ISBN: 9789369549887

First edition 2025

CONTENTS

CHAPTER 1

I hear the voices of people, murmurs and low conversations blending into a muted hum. The sound of footsteps, rhythmic and continuous, streams into my ears like a chorus, an indistinguishable melody. The scent of disinfectant, sharp and sterile, invades my nostrils, making everything feel even more foreign. I can feel the cool air around me, but my body feels heavy, numb. Slowly, as if pushing through a fog, I begin to open my eyes. At first, the white light above me is blinding, its harsh glare forcing my eyelids to flutter shut again. But as I gather strength, my vision starts to clear. The world around me sharpens, yet something still feels... wrong. I try to move, but my body feels like it's not entirely mine. I notice my right hand attached to an IV line, a clear fluid steadily dripping into my veins. My right leg is wrapped in a bandage, stretching up to my knee, and my left arm is also covered, though I can't quite tell why. The feeling of being trapped in my own body begins to sink in, and I try to push aside the rising panic.

I see a figure approaching me, a woman walking quickly toward my bed. She looks familiar, but at the same time, she doesn't as I'm unable to recognize her.

Her expression is clouded with distress, and as she reaches my side, she says, her voice breaking, "Ronnie, I cannot look at you in this condition." The words register, but I feel nothing. I don't understand why she's speaking to me as though I should know who she is. I blink a few times, trying to clear the fog in my head, and ask, "Who is Ronnie, and who are you?"

The words leave my mouth, and almost immediately, the woman freezes. Her face goes pale, her lips trembling, and tears start to pour from her eyes. She looks as though she's been struck by some unimaginable blow. I can't understand why. I didn't mean to upset her; I was simply asking a question. But she doesn't seem to know how to respond. A doctor approaches, seemingly in response to her distress, and she turns to him, her voice frantic as she says, "I am Sandhya, his mother. Why is he not able to recognize me?"

As soon as I hear the words, something clicks in my mind. Sandhya—my mother? But I don't remember her. I don't remember being her son. How can I not remember her? How could I forget my own mother? Overwhelmed by the weight of this realization, I start to question everything. I overhear the doctor speaking to her, his voice gentle but firm. "Your son seems to have lost his memory due to the shock from the accident."

Accident? What accident? I don't recall any accident, nor do I remember anything else. Not even the woman standing beside me, who is supposed to be my mother. I try to piece the fragments together, but it's as if they keep slipping through my fingers. My mind feels like it's wrapped in a thick fog, and the more I attempt to grasp onto a memory, the further it pulls away. What happened to me? Why am I here?

The questions swirl in my mind, but nothing makes sense. I close my eyes again, trying to shut out the noise of uncertainty. I tell myself that this must be a dream, that when I open my eyes again, things will be different—clearer. My last thought before drifting away is that surely, this will all end when I wake. I let go, allowing myself to sink into sleep.

The feeling of soft fingers gently running through my hair rouses me. I can feel a warm presence beside me, and as I slowly lift my gaze, I see her—the woman who claimed to be my mother—sitting beside my bed. She is still here. The panic in my chest tightens once again, as I realize that this is not a dream. The fear rises. I look at her, but the recognition I should feel isn't there. Her fingers are tender as they brush through my hair, and I can sense the depth of her care, but it does nothing to evoke the memory of her as my mother. It's like a part of me refuses to connect with her.

She speaks softly, her voice filled with a mix of hope and sadness. "Ronnie, don't worry about anything. I spoke with the doctor; your memory will come back to you soon." Her words hang in the air, but I don't feel the comfort they're meant to offer. I look at her, searching her face for something familiar, something to anchor me to the truth of who I am. I open my mouth to speak, but the words come out as a murmur. "Hopefully soon." She smiles faintly, but I can see the sorrow behind her eyes, the worry that doesn't fully leave her face. She gently pats my hand and informs me that I'll be discharged in two days. Then, we can go home.

A nurse enters, carrying a tray with food and medication, setting it on the table beside my bed. The scent of the bland food doesn't stir any hunger within me; in fact, the appetite I had moments ago fades as I look at the tray. It feels like a task—just something to get through. I stare at the food for a moment, the taste of blandness in the air before I reluctantly pick up the fork. My mother notices my hesitation and gently says, "Ronnie, you should eat for your recovery."

I nod, but my stomach still feels tight. She doesn't wait for me to respond; instead, she reaches for the food herself, carefully feeding me with her hands. The soft, tender way she does this feels different, more comforting than the cold, sterile food from the tray. Somehow, the food tastes better in her hands, though I know it's the same. It's not the food that makes it taste better; it's the care, the love. The magic of her touch, the warmth that surrounds me even in this cold hospital room, begins to work its way through me. And for a moment, I let myself believe that maybe, just maybe, everything will be okay.

CHAPTER 2

RETURN TO BANGALORE

Getting out of the car, I am greeted by the sight of a large villa, a sprawling structure that, according to my mother, is supposedly my home. The facade is elegant, with tall windows gleaming under the late afternoon sun and a garden out front, the scent of fresh flowers mingling in the air. Yet, everything feels unfamiliar. The weight of not recognizing my surroundings presses against me. My legs feel heavy as I move towards the door, even with the crutches wedged between my arms and legs. The house stood as a silent mystery, and I hesitated for a moment before stepping inside.

The interior of the house is just as grand as the outside. Tall ceilings, expansive rooms, and walls adorned with portraits. Some of the portraits display me, while others show my mother. Yet, nothing feels familiar, nothing feels like it's truly mine. As I step further into the house, I notice one particular portrait set at a distance on the opposite wall—a man's face, garlanded and framed in a place of honor. I stop, unable to place him, and turn to my mother, who's standing nearby. "Who is the man in that photo frame?" I ask, my voice unsure.

She looks at me, her eyes softening with what seems like a mixture of sadness and understanding. She pauses before speaking, as if gathering her thoughts. "He is your father, Ronnie," she says. "He passed away when you were 10 years old."

I stare at the photograph, my mind trying to grasp the weight of her words. It sinks in me slowly—I do not have a father. The thought, though it feels strange, seems to fit. I don't remember him, and there's no sharp ache of loss, no pang of grief that might come from the memory of someone I truly knew. It feels as if a part of me is missing, but I can't quite bring myself to mourn what I don't remember.

I turn away from the photo, trying to shake off the emptiness that threatens to swallow me. I make my way to the living room, where I sit down on the large sofa. Its soft fabric cool beneath my fingertips, though it doesn't offer the comfort I hoped for. My mind is still racing with questions, none of them answered or making sense. Just as I start to lose myself in thought, I hear footsteps approaching. Two people walk into the house, their voices low, but filled with excitement.

I look at them, unsure of who they are. "Who are you?" I ask them, my voice tentative. "Can I help you with something?"

At my question, they both burst into laughter, loud and easy, as if I'd cracked some sort of a joke. I don't understand the humor. My face tightens in confusion, my eyes searching their faces for any clue. Why are they laughing? What did I miss?

Through their laughter, they manage to speak. "Ronnie, are you trying to pull our legs?" one of them says, continuing to laugh, the sound echoing in the room. But my confusion only deepens. Who are they to me? Why does their laughter feel so strange?

Before I can respond, my mother enters the room, her voice soft as she says something to the two men. She gestures towards the dining hall, leading them away from me, but I can still hear the low murmur of their voices. The words don't reach my ears, though—they sound muffled, as if they're just out of reach. I strain to catch them, but nothing makes sense. It's as if their conversation is happening in another world, one I don't belong to.

After exchanging a few words, the two men approach me again, their faces now imprinted with shock. My mother follows behind them, silent, watching from a distance. The men stand in front of me, their eyes wide, filled with a mix of disbelief and sorrow. It's then that I notice the tears, rolling slowly down their cheeks.

"Do you actually not recognize us?" they ask in unison, the shock evident in their voices. There's a painful silence as they wait for my response, and I sense that this moment holds more weight for them than I can understand. A thought suddenly hits me—these men must have been close to me. They must have meant a lot to me, for them to react this way.

I swallow hard before responding, my voice quieter this time, as I try to make sense of it all. "No," I say, "I do not know who you both are, but you can tell me now."

They exchange a glance, a look of confirmation passing between them, before turning back to me. "We are your best friends, Aadi and Dhruv," one of them says, his voice heavy with emotion. "We've been with you since childhood."

There is no rush of feelings and fragmented images flooding my mind. I jog my mind for any trace of them, I can't seem to find anything I can recall about them. They tell me stories—funny, carefree moments we shared, filled with laughter and mischief. Despite the gaping hole in my memory, their words bring a smile to my face, and I can't help but laugh along with them, even though not a single moment they describe sounds familiar.

Their laughter and stories fill the room, and for a while, I forget the emptiness I've been carrying with me. It's as if, at this moment, I'm not alone in my confusion. The warmth of their friendship, the joy in their voices, fills the void where my memories should be, and for a brief moment, I feel a little lighter. But soon, the conversation ends, and they prepare to leave.

I watch them go, the door closing softly behind them, and an unexplainable sense of loss washes over me. My mind feels exhausted, like it's been running for miles without rest. I want nothing more than to lie down, to escape the weight of all these questions, but as I make a move to rest on the sofa, my mother approaches.

"Ronnie," she says, her voice gentle. "Let me help you to your room. You can lie down on your bed comfortably and rest."

I nod, grateful for her presence. She guides me gently toward the stairs, her hand steady on my arm. As we ascend, I notice two rooms facing each other. One must be mine, and the other, I assume, is hers. My mother takes me to the room on the left, the one that's supposed to be mine, and I step inside. The bed looks soft, inviting, but the air in the room is cool and unsettling.

I lie down on the bed, sinking into its softness, but comfort still eludes me. The questions swirl in my mind, yet I try to close my eyes and seek refuge in sleep. My mother's voice drifts in from the doorway. "Ronnie, if you need anything, just call me," she says.

I barely respond, offering only a faint nod in the direction of her voice. She leaves, the door closing behind her. I close my eyes, seeking the calm that sleep should bring, but just as my body begins to relax, a sharp pain pierces through my head. It feels like a storm raging inside my mind, a thousand images rushing towards me all at once. They're blurry, disjointed—flashes of memories, flashes of something I should remember. But they don't come together. The pain deepens, clouding my mind with visions.

CHAPTER 3

VISION

It was a fine evening, the sun just beginning to dip below the horizon, casting a warm glow across the sky. As I stepped out of my house, the crisp air greeted me, filled with the sweet smell of freshly cut grass and the faint scent of gasoline. Following the scent, I saw my dad working on his bike, his hands covered in grease. His face was lit with joy, his brow furrowed in concentration; there was an unmistakable smile that tugged at the corners of his lips whenever he was around his bike, as he is now.

I approached him slowly, unsure if I was interrupting something important. "Dad, can I help with anything?" I asked, my voice filled with curiosity.

He looked up at me, his smile widening. "Yes, Ronnie, you can pass me those tools," he replied, pointing to the toolbox beside me.

I nodded eagerly, moving to grab the tools he needed. There was something almost magical about the way my dad seemed when he was working on his bike. It was as if the bike had a special place in his heart, a place I couldn't quite understand but felt a deep sense of affection for. As I handed him a wrench, I couldn't help but ask, "Dad, why are you so connected with this bike? I see a smile on your face whenever you're around it."

He paused for a moment, wiping his hands on a rag before looking at me. His eyes softened, and I could see a nostalgic gleam in them. "Ronnie, this is the first bike I ever bought. I've had it for years, and it holds a lot of memories. Your mother and I, we shared so many good times on this bike—trips, laughter, and just being together. Every time I'm around it, those pleasant memories flood my mind."

I nodded, trying to understand what he meant. "Oh, yes! This is the same bike on which you made Mom fall in love with you, right?" I said, a teasing smile spreading across my face.

His face lit up, and he laughed softly. "Yes, son, this is the same bike. Now you know why it's so dear to me."

The connection he had with that bike was evident. It wasn't just a means of transportation for him—it was a symbol of something much greater, a bridge between the past and present, filled with memories of a love shared between him and my mother. I stood there with him, both of us immersed in that moment, sharing a bond without words. The evening passed quickly, the last rays of the sun disappearing into the horizon, allowing the moon's bright white light to cast a calming glow over the scene.

"Looks like the bike is ready," my dad said, wiping his hands on a rag one final time. "Ronnie, I'll take you out on a ride tomorrow evening."

Excitement surged through me at the thought. "Sure, Dad, that sounds like fun!" I replied, already imagining the joy of riding alongside him, the wind rushing past us, and the freedom that came with being on the open road.

The next day, I woke up to the familiar tune of the morning alarm. But today felt different—there was a sense of excitement in the air that wasn't there on other days. I could hardly contain my anticipation for the evening. It wasn't just an ordinary day; it was the day I would be spending time with my dad, riding the bike we had worked on together the previous evening. I hurried through my morning routine, my mind already racing toward the evening ahead.

As I walked into school, my friend Dhruv spotted me from a distance. He jogged over with a smile on his face. "Hey, Ronnie! What's up?" he asked, clearly in a good mood.

"My dad finally got his bike running," I said, my voice filled with excitement. "He promised he'd take me for a ride this evening."

Dhruv's face lit up at the news. "Nice, Ronnie! Looks like you're going to have a blast tonight!"

I grinned, my excitement mirrored on his face. "Yeah, I can't wait! It's going to be so much fun."

The rest of the school day passed in a blur. I was practically counting down the minutes until the final bell rang. Every class felt like it dragged on forever, my mind wandering to thoughts of the bike ride, of spending time with my dad, feeling the wind against my face as we sped down the road. The anticipation was almost unbearable.

Finally, the school day ended. The bell rang, signaling the end of the last class. Without a second thought, I rushed out of the classroom, my feet barely touching the ground as I made my way home. I couldn't wait to see my dad, to get ready for the ride that had been promised.

But when I arrived home, something felt... off. There were people gathered outside and inside the house. The front door was wide open, and I could hear murmurs of conversation, hushed voices filled with uncertainty. My heart began to race, the excitement of the day quickly replaced by a sense of unease. I walked slowly into the house, unsure of what was happening.

The first thing that caught my eye was my dad, lying motionless on the wooden cot, placed in the living room. My mother stood nearby, her face pale, her eyes filled with tears. I froze in my tracks, my breath caught in my throat. My mind tried to process the scene, but nothing made sense.

I moved towards my dad, my legs shaking. "Dad?" I called out, my voice trembling. "Dad, wake up."

I shook his body gently, trying to rouse him, but he remained lifeless, unresponsive. Panic began to set in as I tried harder, desperation taking hold of me. "Dad, why won't you wake up?" I asked, my voice rising in fear.

My mother, her eyes red and swollen from crying, approached me slowly, her expression full of pain. She reached out, placing a trembling hand on my shoulder. "Ronnie," she said softly, her voice breaking. "Your dad is no more."

The words hit me like a slap, and the world around me started spinning out of control. No, this couldn't be real. It couldn't be happening. My mind refused to accept what she was saying. I shook my head in disbelief. "What do you mean, Mom? Dad promised me he'd take me on a ride today! He's not gone, he can't be!"

Tears began to well up in my eyes as I tried to make sense of it all. Then, I heard the hushed voices of the people gathered around us. "He passed away from a heart attack," one voice said. "He was too young… so much left undone."

Those words echoed in my ears, forming a dreadful chorus in my mind. I tried to push them away, but they clung to me, suffocating me with their finality. My dad, the man I looked up to, the one I was supposed to share a ride with, was gone. And I couldn't understand why or how. My world felt like it had shattered into a thousand pieces, leaving me standing amidst the wreckage, unable to pick them up.

PRESENT

I jolted awake, gasping for air as I opened my eyes, my heart pounding in my chest. My breath came in short, frantic gasps, and for a moment, I couldn't tell if I was still dreaming or if I had woken up. The remains of the nightmare clung to me, lingering like a fog, clouding my thoughts.

"Mom! Mom!" I called out loudly, my voice echoing in the silence of my room. The fear that had overtaken me in the dream was still gripping my heart, and I couldn't shake it off. I needed my mother, needed her to tell me that everything was okay.

Within moments, I heard the sound of hurried footsteps, and my mother rushed into the room. Her face was full of concern, eyes wide with worry. "What happened, Ronnie? Is everything okay?" she asked, her voice trembling slightly.

I could barely speak, my chest tight with emotion. "I… I had a bad dream," I whispered, my voice hoarse.

She sat beside me on the bed, pulling me into a tight embrace. Her arms were warm and comforting, yet despite her steady presence, the fear in my heart didn't dissipate. Tears began to fall, and I couldn't stop them. The weight of the nightmare, of the loss, was too much to bear.

As I cried, I wiped my tears away, my mind still reeling from the vivid images of my father's death. "Mom," I said, my voice shaking. "When… when did Dad pass away? How did it happen?"

My mother sighed, her voice soft and gentle as she began to recount the events. The words she spoke felt like a dagger to my heart. They mirrored exactly what I had seen in the nightmare—the heart attack, the suddenness with which it occurred, the shock of losing him. As her words faded, I was knocked out of the blue, overwhelmed by the crushing reality.

CHAPTER 4

FEW WEEKS LATER

The clouds were gracing the sky, their jovial drops dotting the earth below as they seemed to dance with the wind. The mountains stood proudly in the distance, their green peaks forming a stunning backdrop against the grey sky. It was a sight so peaceful, so calming, that it felt like a reward to the soul. The lush greenery surrounding the area breathed life into the space, and the stillness made everything feel more real. I sat on my bike, watching this beautiful scene unfold before me, utterly immersed in the tranquility of the moment. The scent of fresh rain mixed with earth, filling the air with a pure aroma that made it seem as if time had slowed down just for me.

It was at that moment, as I soaked in the tranquility of the natural world around me, that I felt a hand on my shoulder. The touch was soft yet firm, pulling me out of the serenity I had been lost in. As I turned my head toward my shoulder, I heard my name being called, a voice that was both familiar and comforting, yet somehow felt distant, almost surreal. "Ronnie, Ronnie, Ronnie…" the voice called, followed by, "Get up, you will get late for college."

A feeling of confusion washed over me, as the voice and the hand grew stronger, as if urging me to wake up. I closed my eyes for a moment, attempting to hold onto the peace I had just experienced, but as I opened them again, the scenery shifted. I found myself back in my room, lying on my bed, with my mother standing beside me. The soft morning light filtered through the curtains, casting a gentle glow over everything.

"Ronnie, get up," my mother repeated, her voice filled with warmth yet gentle urgency. "You don't want to be late for your first day."

I rubbed my eyes, still in a haze, trying to piece together what had just happened. My dream felt so real, so vivid, that for a moment I wasn't sure if I was still asleep. But reality began to settle in as my mother's words sank in. "First day," I mumbled to myself. I hadn't even realized it, but today was the day that my college journey was about to begin. My mind was swirling with thoughts, none of which felt quite at home, and yet here I was, about to step into a new chapter of my life.

With a deep sigh, I pushed myself out of bed, my mind still trying to shake the remains of the strange dream. I stumbled toward the bathroom to take a quick shower, attempting to clear my head. The sound of water rushing over me seemed to wash away some of the fog, and I slowly began to feel more awake. As I dried off and wrapped a towel around myself, I stepped back into my room to find a neatly pressed set of clothes laid out on the bed. My mother had already taken care of the details. Her presence in my life was comforting, but something in me still felt unsettled.

When I came downstairs, the rich aroma of breakfast greeted me. My mother was busy setting the dining table, moving gracefully between the stove and the counter, her movements effortless and comforting. She looked up as I entered the kitchen and smiled warmly.

"Ronnie, come have a seat," she said, her voice always filled with love. "I'll serve you breakfast."

I sat down at the table, the smells of idli, vada, chutney filling the air, making my stomach growl with anticipation. The food looked delicious as it was placed before me, and I couldn't help but take a bite almost immediately.

"Mom, you make the best food in the world," I said, savoring the flavors in my mouth. She smiled, her eyes lighting up with pride, and asked, "Ronnie, are you excited for your first day at college?"

I nodded, though my mind was a whirlwind of conflicting emotions. "Yes," I said aloud, trying to sound more confident than I felt. But inside, I was still struggling with the pieces of my life that didn't seem to fit together. The memories of my time at the hospital, the unsettling vision, and the strange sense of disconnection came onto me. I couldn't shake the feeling that something was missing, something crucial that I needed to understand. My mind kept drifting back to the vision I had—of my father, a terrifying image that still haunted me. Yet, there was no explanation, no clarity. Only fragments of confusion.

My mother placed a warm hand on my shoulder, breaking my train of thought. "Good luck, Ronnie," she said softly. "You'll do great. Love you."

"Love you too, Mom," I replied, hugging her tightly before heading out the door.

As I made my way to college, the cool morning air hit my face, a welcome contrast to the heat I had felt in the kitchen. My heart pounded in my chest with excitement and nerves mixed into one. College. It was supposed to be an exciting new chapter, right? A fresh start. But I still couldn't shake the feeling that something wasn't quite right. When I finally arrived at the college campus, it was bustling with energy. Students were chatting in groups, some hurrying between buildings, while others sat under trees, engrossed in their phones or books. It was the kind of atmosphere I had imagined—lively and full of new beginnings—but somehow it felt distant, like I was standing on the outside, looking in.

I walked across the campus, trying to focus on finding my classroom. The chatter of students filled the air, but my thoughts were far away, tangled in confusion. The noise seemed to fade into the background as I became absorbed in my search for directions. Finally, I spotted a board with directions to various classrooms. After scanning it for a moment, I located the room I was looking for and followed the signs.

The classroom door opened with a soft creak, and I stepped inside, scanning the room for a place to sit. There were many new faces, all talking and laughing, but none of them seemed familiar. I felt out of place, like I was drifting in a sea of people who were all on a different wavelength. Not wanting to interact, I quickly made my way to an empty seat by the window and slid into it, hoping to disappear into the background.

The bell rang, signaling the start of the class, and the professor walked in with a warm smile, ready to begin. I tried to focus on the class, but my mind kept drifting elsewhere. My eyes wandered over to the window, where I watched the trees sway in the wind. The soft rustling of leaves outside provided a kind of rhythm, a calming sound, but it didn't last long. Suddenly, the peaceful scenery outside the window morphed into something else—something familiar, yet horrifying.

In an instant, I was no longer in the classroom. The thoughts were so vivid, so real, that I felt like I was back in that place, trapped in the scene once again. The buzz of the classroom faded away. I saw a figure—my father—his face contorted in pain, and then… it was gone. The image faded, leaving me breathless, my heart racing as if I had just experienced it for real. I blinked rapidly, trying to shake off the vision, but it clung to me, stubborn and persistent.

I looked around, my surroundings now blurry, as if I was still caught between two worlds—one where I sat in a college classroom, and another where the past still haunted me. My chest tightened, and I tried to calm myself, focusing on my breath as I forced myself to return to the present. I had to keep it together.

But the images in my mind, the hazy remnants of memories, refused to fade. Every time I closed my eyes, they would return, like ghosts lurking in the back of my mind, reminding me that something was wrong. My first day at college was supposed to be a fresh start, but I couldn't escape the nagging feeling that I was carrying something with me—something I couldn't remember, but something that shaped who I was.

I glanced around the room again, looking at the faces of my classmates, and for the first time, I felt truly alone in a crowd. The life I thought I knew felt like a distant memory, and I was left to navigate this new reality, trying to find pieces of myself in a world that felt both familiar and foreign. And in that moment, I couldn't help but wonder: would I ever truly find the answers I was seeking? Would I ever understand the truth of what had happened to me? As these questions hovered over my mind, I found myself slipping into another vision.

CHAPTER 5

VISION

It was a beautiful Sunday morning—the kind of morning when the sun lazily climbed higher in the sky, casting a warm, golden light through the curtains of my room. I opened my eyes and stretched out, feeling the comfort of the soft bed beneath me, the perfect contrast to the busy week I had left behind. I could hear the faintest sounds coming from the kitchen—the clinking of pots and pans, the sizzling of food being cooked. My stomach growled in anticipation as the scent of something delicious reached my nose. I could almost taste the flavors in the air, and it instantly made me feel at home, safe, and cared for.

I threw the blankets off and got out of bed, following the inviting aroma towards the kitchen. But when I stepped into the room, I froze. The kitchen was empty. Not a single sign of the food I had been dreaming of, no ingredients out on the counter, no pots simmering on the stove. The space was quiet and devoid of any sign of life, except for the refrigerator humming in the corner. I stood there for a moment, confused, the strange but comforting scent still lingering in my senses. I closed my eyes and inhaled deeply, following the smell like a breadcrumb trail.

Curious and half-amused, I stepped outside the kitchen, still trying to make sense of it all. My eyes drifted across the hallway, and I soon realized where the scent was coming from—my neighbor's house. They must have been cooking something delicious, and the fragrance was drifting through the walls, as if inviting me to join in. I chuckled to myself, not surprised in the least. This kind of thing seemed to happen often—our neighbors' kitchen always smelled better than ours on the weekends.

I started to walk back toward the living room when I caught sight of my mom sitting on the couch, her eyes glued to the TV screen. She was watching one of those spooky horror movies where the tension builds slowly, and every little sound makes you jump. At that moment, the character on screen was in a dimly lit room, and the camera panned slowly to show a ghostly figure right behind them. The music swelled, and the character started to turn around slowly, about to face what could only be the terrifying figure of a spirit. My mom sat there, totally engrossed, eyes wide, waiting for the horror to unfold.

I saw my chance.

With a mischievous grin on my face, I crept up behind her, moving as quietly as I could. When I was just inches away, I leaped and let out the loudest noise I could make, right next to her ear.

She screamed, the high-pitched sound cutting through the silence, and I burst out laughing immediately. "You naughty kid, my heart skipped a beat there!" she said, her hand pressed to her chest as she tried to regain her composure.

"Sorry, Mom," I said, still laughing. "But it sure was fun."

She shook her head, her lips curling into a playful smirk. "Yeah, sure, it was fun for you," she teased. "But I wish I could say the same."

I plopped down beside her, still chuckling. After a moment, I glanced at the kitchen and then back at her. "Mom, why is there no meal prepared in the kitchen?"

She raised an eyebrow and gave me a look, clearly not expecting that question. "Well, I was waiting for my sweet son to rise and make something," she replied with a grin.

I sighed dramatically. "Ugh, well, it's Sunday, Mom. I want to kick back and watch something, not cook."

She leaned back on the couch, a playful glow in her eyes. "Well, it's Sunday for me too, Ronnie."

I rolled my eyes and crossed my arms. "Fine, my dear mother. I'll whip up some eggs and cheese sandwiches for us."

"Thank you, sweetie," she said with a smile, before returning her attention to the TV screen.

I headed to the kitchen, opening the fridge to gather the necessary ingredients, but when I checked the egg carton, I found it empty. My stomach growled again, but this time, it was accompanied by a sense of mild frustration. "Great," I muttered to myself, "we're out of eggs."

"Be right back!" I called out to my mom, "I'm going to the store to grab some eggs."

I slipped on my shoes and stepped out of the house, heading to the corner store. As I walked down the sidewalk, I spotted a familiar figure riding towards me on a bike. It was Aadi, my childhood friend. I waved him down, and he slowed to a stop beside me.

"Hey, Ronnie! What's up?" Aadi greeted me with his usual grin.

"I'm off to buy some eggs. Want to come with me?" I asked.

He groaned, rolling his eyes. "Ugh, it seems like I always show up at the wrong time. You always manage to drag me along for your errands," he whined.

I laughed. "Well, come on, you're already here."

Aadi's face lit up. "Alright, alright. I'll come, but you owe me big time for this," he said.

"Deal," I agreed, laughing as I grabbed his spare helmet and hopped on behind him.

The ride to the store was quick, and soon enough, I was holding a bag of eggs and a small pack of chips. I handed Aadi the bag of chips with a grin.

"For your tantrum earlier," I joked.

He laughed. "Well, at least I got a free snack out of it."

As we stopped in front of my house, I turned to Aadi. "Come on in and have some eggs," I offered.

Aadi shook his head. "I want to, but my girlfriend's waiting for me. She'll kill me if I get late," he said, a look of mock terror on his face.

I raised an eyebrow and smirked. "Okay, you wouldn't want to make your lovebird angry. Bye, Aadi."

He waved at me as he rode off, and I headed inside with the eggs in hand.

As I entered the house, I made my way to the kitchen, placing the eggs on the counter and pulling out the other ingredients for the sandwiches. The smell of sizzling eggs and melted cheese soon filled the kitchen, and before long, the delicious aroma wafted out into the living room. My mom, still seated on the couch, took notice.

"Wow, Ronnie, what have you made? It smells really good!" she called out, her voice full of genuine surprise and excitement.

I glanced up from the stove with a smile. "Just a simple egg and cheese sandwich," I said, flipping the sandwich in the pan to make sure it was perfectly golden on both sides.

I plated the sandwiches and walked over to her. She took a bite, savoring the flavors, and her face lit up with appreciation.

"Wow, Ronnie," she said, her mouth still full. "This is delicious."

I sat down next to her, finally able to relax a little. "Glad you like it, Mom," I said, smiling. "I've been meaning to ask you something."

She looked at me, intrigued. "What is it, sweetie?"

"Can I go on a solo road trip before college starts?" I asked, my voice tinged with a mixture of excitement and uncertainty. "I just need to clear my head, get away for a little while, and experience something new before diving into all the pressure that's coming with college."

Her face softened as she considered my request. "Sure, sweetie," she said without hesitation. "What place have you got in mind?"

I thought for a moment, then shrugged. "I haven't decided yet. I just want to go somewhere, anywhere. I'll figure it out once I hit the road."

She nodded, understanding my need for some time alone. "So when are you planning on going?" she asked.

"I was thinking of leaving tomorrow morning," I said. "I want to get an early start and be back by Thursday."

"Okay," she said, a gentle smile tugging at her lips. "Have fun and enjoy, but be safe."

I smiled gratefully at her, feeling a rush of both relief and excitement all at once. I had her blessing, and now I could finally set out on this adventure, even if it was just for a few days.

Later that night, after dinner and a long conversation with my mom, I went to my room and began to prepare for the trip. I pulled a bag out of my closet and began to pack clothes and essentials—t-shirts, a pair of jeans, my toiletries, and a few other things I thought I might need. I laid out my riding gear on the couch: my leather jacket, helmet, and gloves. The thought of hitting the open road on my bike gave me an indescribable thrill, and I couldn't wait to set out on my own.

Before going to bed, I set the alarm for four o'clock in the morning. I needed to get a good night's rest before the journey ahead. As I lay down in bed, my mind raced with anticipation. The road trip would be a much-needed escape—a way to clear my mind, to find some clarity before the whirlwind of college life began. I closed my eyes and drifted off to sleep, the excitement of tomorrow's adventure pervading my dreams.

CHAPTER 6

The bell's sharp ring abruptly pulled me out of my vision. The world around me slowly refocused as the sound of the bell echoed through the hall, signaling the end of class and the start of a brief break. I blinked a couple of times to shake off the lingering effects of the vision I had just experienced. The strange and cryptic imagery still swirled around in my thoughts, and I struggled to make sense of it. It was as if my mind had been swept away to another world, leaving me with more questions than answers. I hadn't even realized the class had ended.

A voice brought me back to the present. I turned to find a guy standing beside me, offering a friendly smile. "Hi, I'm Mahesh," he said, extending his hand in greeting.

I blinked a few times, still processing the vision, but managed a smile and shook his hand. "Hi Mahesh, I'm Ronnie."

"It's break time now," Mahesh continued. "We're heading to the canteen. Do you want to join us?"

I paused for a moment, my mind still caught in the haze of the vision. A break sounded like exactly what I needed, something to take my mind off my thoughts for a bit. I nodded and said, "Sure, I'll join."

I didn't know my way around the campus yet, but Mahesh seemed friendly, and he was with a group of others. I figured I'd just follow them and hope I didn't get too lost. We started walking through the bustling college hallways, and I did my best to take in my surroundings. The campus was large, with students rushing in all directions. The chatter and laughter around me created a lively atmosphere, one that felt starkly different from the quiet world I had been lost in moments before.

As we walked, Mahesh turned to me with a kind smile. "Ronnie, do you want anything to eat or drink while we're at the canteen?"

I thought about it for a moment. "No, I'm good, thanks," I replied. My stomach wasn't particularly hungry, and my mind was still preoccupied with the visions I'd experienced earlier. I wasn't sure why, but it seemed to hold some deeper meaning that I couldn't quite grasp. It was frustrating.

The canteen was a large, open space with long tables and an array of food stalls. The smell of freshly cooked food filled the air, and I couldn't help but feel a little more grounded in this bustling environment. The noise and energy of the place distracted me from the storm of thoughts swirling in my mind. I followed Mahesh and the others to a table and sat down.

As I settled into my seat, I tried to shake off the feeling that something important was slipping through my fingers, but it was hard to focus on anything else. Just then, Mahesh introduced me to the others sitting at the table: Ram, Karan, and Shruthi. They all smiled at me warmly.

"Hey Ronnie, welcome to the group!" Ram said with a grin.

"Yeah, don't worry. We don't bite!" Karan added, chuckling.

Shruthi, who had been quietly observing me, tilted her head and said with a playful smile, "You know all of our names, but we still don't know yours. Should we just call you 'handsome'?"

I couldn't help but laugh at her teasing. "Well, I suppose I can't blame you for that. I'm Ronnie," I said, smiling back at her.

The laughter at the table grew a bit louder, and the lighthearted banter made me feel more at ease. As the conversation flowed, I found myself momentarily forgetting about the unsettling visions that had been clouding my mind all day. It felt good to be around people, to engage in small talk and jokes that made the world feel a little more normal. My new friends seemed easygoing, and for the first time since I arrived at college, I felt like maybe this place wouldn't be so bad after all.

We chatted for a while longer, exchanging stories of our first days on campus, laughing at the awkward moments and sharing little quirks about college life. For the most part, I was able to put the strange visions on hold for some time. The noise and bustle of the canteen helped clear my head, and I focused on enjoying the company of my new friends. It was a welcome distraction.

By the time the break was over, I had learned quite a bit about my new friends. Mahesh was a history buff, Ram was passionate about photography, Karan was into music, and Shruthi was a fan of adventure sports. It was nice to be surrounded by people who seemed to have such diverse interests. But as soon as we parted ways to head back to our classes, my mind kept drifting back to those images. They were still with me, hovering at the edges of my thoughts, as though they were waiting for the right moment to reveal their meaning.

Even when I got home later that evening, the visions refused to leave my mind. The day had been full of new experiences and new people, but the strange images overshadowed everything else, persistent and inescapable. I needed a break from thinking about it, so I decided to just relax in front of the television. Maybe a movie or a TV show would help distract my mind.

As I settled into the living room and turned on the TV, my mom walked in after a long day at work. "Hi, sweetie," she greeted me with a tired but warm smile.

"Hi, Mom," I replied, offering her a smile in return.

She asked, "So, how was your first day at college?"

"It was nice," I said, settling back into the couch. "I made a couple of friends. It wasn't as nerve-wracking as I thought it would be."

"That's great to hear," she said, her tone lightening. "I'm glad you're getting along with people. So, what's the plan for dinner?"

I grinned. "How about we order biryani?"

Mom raised an eyebrow. "Biryani? You're really craving that, huh? Alright, I'll freshen up, and you can order it while I get changed."

"Okay, sounds good," I said, already reaching for my phone to place the order.

As I pulled up the food delivery app, my attention was drawn to the TV, where a scene from a movie showed the main character on a road trip. The character was riding his bike down a long, winding road that seemed to stretch on forever. It was a beautiful shot, with the landscape sprawling out beneath a setting sun. The moment was serene, but something about it seemed to trigger something in my mind.

Suddenly, the vision I had earlier returned, this time more vivid and unsettling. The images in my head were of a similar road, a long and endless stretch of highway that I had never seen before. Yet itd seemed familiar in a way that didn't make sense, as though I had traveled it before, even though I knew I hadn't. My heart began to race, and a strange feeling washed over me, as if I was being pulled into a memory that didn't belong to me. I couldn't understand it, but the images were as clear as day, flashing before my eyes in rapid succession.

I felt a chill run down my spine. This was no random vision; it felt like something more. My mind was trying to tell me something, but what? I closed my eyes for a moment, trying to steady my breathing. The images were still there, flickering at the edges of my mind, but now they were accompanied by a sense of urgency.

"Ronnie, are you okay?" My mom's voice broke through my thoughts, and I blinked, finding her standing in the doorway, her eyes concerned.

"Uh, yeah, Mom, I'm fine," I said quickly, trying to shake off the unsettling feeling. "Just… I don't know. I guess I'm a little tired."

"Well, go ahead and place the order, and we can eat and relax. You've had a long day."

"Yeah, sure," I replied, taking a deep breath to calm myself.

As I focused on placing the order, I couldn't help but feel like something strange was beginning to unfold. The visions, the feeling of déjà vu, the road trip on the TV—it all seemed too connected to ignore. But what did it mean? What was my mind trying to tell me? I wasn't sure yet, but one thing was certain: this was just the beginning. Something bigger was coming, and I could feel it in my bones. Another vision flashes in my head, this one sharp and clear.

CHAPTER 7

VISION

I was cruising down the highway on my bike, feeling the gentle breeze against my face as I took in the vast expanse of the sky above me. The sun had just begun its descent, painting the sky in shades of pink, orange, and purple. The beauty of the moment was something I wanted to savor, so I slowed down my bike, allowing myself to fully appreciate the serenity that surrounded me. As I rode, I thought about how much I enjoyed these quiet moments of peace, away from the chaos of everyday life. There was something therapeutic about the open road, the wind flowing through me, and the rhythmic hum of the bike beneath me.

Soon, I felt the familiar rumble in my stomach, reminding me that it was time for lunch. I decided to stop at a nearby restaurant, and my eyes scanned the road for a place that looked inviting. After a few moments, I spotted a charming little restaurant tucked away just off the side of the highway. It had a welcoming vibe, with a small sign that read "Spice Symphony." It looked like the perfect place to take a break and enjoy a meal.

I parked my bike in the lot, removed my helmet, and took a deep breath of fresh air. The cool breeze and the smell of the surrounding nature felt refreshing after being on the road for a while. I made my way towards the restaurant, and as soon as I stepped through the door, I was greeted by a blast of cool air from the air conditioning. It felt like a much-needed relief from the afternoon heat. The interior of the restaurant was cozy, with soft lighting and wooden furniture that gave the place a warm, homely feel. There was a calm ambiance that made me instantly relax.

A waitress approached me with a friendly smile, and I couldn't help but notice how her positive energy immediately brightened the atmosphere. "Welcome to Spice Symphony! How can I help you today?" she asked cheerfully.

I returned her smile and said, "Wow, you have a wonderful smile." The compliment seemed to catch her off guard, and she blushed slightly before replying, "Oh, thank you!" Her smile widened, and she looked pleased by the compliment.

She continued, "Table for how many?"

"Just one, please," I replied.

"Follow me," she said, leading me toward an empty table. As we walked, I passed by other diners, who seemed to be enjoying their meals. The sound of forks clinking against plates, along with the low hum of conversation, created a warm and inviting atmosphere. I thought to myself that this place must be good if it was attracting so many happy customers. I felt excited about the meal

I was about to have and hoped it would be one I would remember for a long time.

The waitress led me to a table near a large glass wall, giving me a view of the garden outside. I sat down and noticed her name tag read "Sonia." She placed a menu in front of me and asked, "Would you like something to drink while you decide?"

I was feeling a bit parched after the ride, so I quickly responded, "A lemonade, please."

"Coming right up," Sonia said, before heading toward the kitchen.

As she walked away, I began browsing the menu, carefully considering my options. The restaurant had a wide range of dishes, from hearty meat-based meals to lighter vegetarian options, but I found myself stopping at the butter chicken section. The description sounded delicious, and I had a craving for something rich and flavorful. I knew I had to try it.

Sonia returned shortly with a glass of lemonade, the refreshing citrus aroma immediately tempting me to take a sip. She set the glass on the table and asked, "Have you decided what you'd like to order?"

I nodded and said, "Yes, I'd like to have the butter chicken with two butter naans, please."

Sonia smiled and jotted down my order in her notepad. "Butter chicken is our specialty," she said with a knowing look. "I'm sure you'll love it."

I couldn't wait. As she walked away to put in the order, I glanced around the restaurant again. The walls were decorated with nature-themed artwork, and the soothing sounds of soft music played in the background. The space felt peaceful, almost like an oasis from the world outside.

My attention was drawn to the glass wall, which offered a beautiful view of a pond outside. The water was calm, with koi fish gliding effortlessly through the surface. I watched them for a while, mesmerized by their graceful movements. The colors of the fish—bright oranges, whites, and blacks—contrasted beautifully against the clear blue water. The sight was soothing, and I found myself getting lost in the peaceful ambiance of the restaurant.

Just as I was beginning to feel completely relaxed, Sonia returned with my meal. She placed a steaming plate of butter chicken in front of me, along with two warm, fluffy butter naans. The aroma of the food hit me immediately, and my stomach growled in anticipation. Sonia smiled and said, "Enjoy your meal," before turning and walking back to her station.

I picked up a piece of naan, dipped it into the rich, creamy butter chicken curry, and took a bite. The flavors were incredible—rich, savory, and comforting all at once. The tender chicken melted in my mouth, and the naan was soft and perfectly cooked, just the way I liked it. I closed my eyes as I savored the taste, completely lost in the moment.

As I was enjoying my meal, a strange sensation washed over me. It felt like the world around me was slowly fading away. Suddenly, the sound of a phone buzzing broke the blissful moment. The buzzing grew louder, and before I knew it, my eyes snapped open. I was no longer sitting at the table in the restaurant, but back in my own bed. The bright sunlight streaming in through the window at the restaurant was replaced by the dark in my room. I reached over to my nightstand and grabbed my phone, turning off the alarm. The time read 4:00 AM.

I sat up, rubbing my eyes and trying to shake off the remnants of the dream. "That was a nice dream," I muttered to myself, still feeling the warmth of the butter chicken in my memory. "That butter chicken must have tasted good." I chuckled softly, still trying to process the strange transition from dream to reality. The dream felt so real, almost as if I had actually been there. It was odd, but at the same time, it felt comforting.

I stood up from the bed, still feeling a bit drowsy. I wiped the sleep from my eyes and headed toward the bathroom to freshen up. The warm water from the shower helped wake me up, and I began to feel more alert. I dressed in the clothes I had set aside the night before and began putting on my riding gear. The excitement of the day ahead slowly crept in, and I couldn't help but feel a sense of anticipation building inside me.

Once I was ready, I grabbed my bag and threw the straps over my shoulders. The weight of the bag was heavier than I expected, and I grunted a little as I adjusted it. It was a little too early for me to be fully awake, but I was determined to get going.

I made my way to my mom's room, intending to say goodbye before heading out. She was still asleep, her soft breathing filling the room. I didn't want to wake her, so I quietly whispered, "Bye, Mom." I slipped out of the house and into the cool early morning air.

My bike was waiting for me outside, and as I started it up, I felt the familiar rush of excitement. There was something refreshing about the early morning hours—the world felt still and peaceful, and the road ahead was full of possibility. I checked my phone, and the time read 5:00 AM. I was eager to begin my journey.

As I rode through the quiet city streets of Bengaluru, a sense of calm descended over me. The city was still asleep, and the roads were empty. As I rode on, I soon found myself on National Highway 44, feeling the wind against my face as I picked up speed. The sky was just beginning to lighten, the first rays of the sun peeking over the horizon. I inhaled deeply, savoring the fresh morning air. There was something incredibly peaceful about the moment. I closed my eyes for a second, letting the calmness of the scene wash over me. The sound of my bike's engine mixed with the gentle breeze, and for a brief moment, it felt like everything was in perfect harmony.

PRESENT

A loud bang from the movie on the TV jolted me out of my vision and back into the present. I quickly turned off the TV. Just then, I saw my mother coming downstairs, looking refreshed. I glanced up from my phone just as she entered the hall. With a smile, she asked, "Did you place the order yet?"

I glanced at the time on my phone and saw that it was already getting late. I hadn't realized how much time had passed while I was lost in thought, trying to decide what

I wanted to order as well as reflecting on the strange and vivid visions I was experiencing. I paused for a moment, feeling distracted by those thoughts, but I quickly turned my attention back to the task at hand. "No, I haven't placed the order yet. I was just searching for a good place to order from," I replied, trying to focus on the practical details of the day.

My mother chuckled lightly and gave me an amused look. "After all that time spent searching for a place to order from, I guess the food better be worth it, right?" she said with a teasing tone, her eyebrows raised slightly in playful judgment.

I smiled back at her, trying to ease the tension of the moment. "Yes, Mom, I'm sure it will be great. The place I'm ordering from has really good reviews. Lots of people recommend it," I said, trying to reassure her that my search wasn't all in vain. The place I had found had been highly rated by a lot of people online, and I had even looked through the reviews to make sure I wasn't making a hasty decision.

As I said this, my thoughts drifted away to something else entirely. The mention of reviews and recommendations triggered something deeper in my mind, and for a moment, I wasn't thinking about the food anymore. Instead, I was thinking about something much more complex—those three visions I had experienced since the accident. The first vision had been about my father, and it felt so real, so true. It wasn't just a vague image or a fleeting moment; it was a memory, a vision of something that felt like it had happened in another life, in another time. I hadn't been able to fully process it at the time, but it had stayed with me— like a piece of my past that had been buried was now resurfacing.

The second vision was vivid, showcasing a jovial moment with my mother. The horror movie that she was watching, the food I made, eggs and cheese sandwich. Every detail from that vision is still crystal clear.

The third vision, the one I had just experienced before waking up this morning, was just as intense. The details were clear in my mind—the restaurant, the waitress, the butter chicken, the glass wall with koi fish swimming peacefully in a pond. And yet, it was just a dream I had before my road trip. The bike I was riding on the trip felt familiar. It had felt like a memory that was trying to break through, trying to tell me something important. And as I thought more about it, I began to wonder: *Could these visions be related?* What if they weren't random or disconnected events, but part of a larger picture—part of a story from my past that I had forgotten?

I paused for a moment, lost in my own thoughts. I hadn't told anyone about the visions yet. They felt too personal, too confusing, and I wasn't sure how to explain them. How could I explain something that didn't make sense, something that seemed both real and impossible at the same time? My mind kept returning to the idea that these visions were connected to memories—memories of a time before the accident, memories I had somehow lost or forgotten.

I shifted uncomfortably on the couch, the weight of the thoughts pulling me deeper into contemplation. The vision of my father was a true event from the past, but what if the other visions were also real? What if it was a glimpse of something that had actually happened? I had always believed that certain memories, especially the ones that were painful or difficult to face, had a way of slipping away from our conscious minds. But these visions felt different. They weren't just fragments of forgotten memories; they felt like pieces of a puzzle that I had never even known existed, pieces that were now starting to fit together.

I looked at my phone again, barely registering the screen. My mind was racing. The vision of the restaurant, the peaceful koi fish, and the waitress named Sonia—it all felt so vivid, so clear. It had to mean something. But the more I tried to piece it together, the more I realized that I couldn't remember enough details to make any sense of it. It was as if the memories were just out of reach, hovering at the edge of my consciousness, waiting for something to trigger them fully.

My mother's voice broke through my reverie. "Are you sure you're okay, sweetie?" she asked, concern evident in her tone. "You've been kind of quiet. Is everything alright?"

I looked up at her and forced a smile. "Yeah, Mom, I'm fine. Just a little tired, that's all," I said, trying to sound more convincing than I felt. "I'll place the order now, don't worry."

She didn't seem entirely convinced, but she nodded and gave me a reassuring pat on the shoulder. "Alright, if you say so. But don't overthink things, okay? It's just food, not the end of the world." She smiled gently at me, clearly trying to lighten the mood.

I nodded, though my mind was still spinning. As I reached for my phone to place the order, I couldn't help but think about how strange it was that these visions were popping up now. Why were they coming to me now, after so long? It didn't make sense, and yet, there was a part of me that felt like I was on the verge of discovering something important. But what?

I glanced at my mother again, who was now busy on her laptop. She seemed so unaware of the turmoil going on inside my mind. I wondered if she would understand if I told her about the visions. But how could I explain them? How could I explain the strange sense of déjà vu that was haunting me?

I rubbed my eyes, trying to clear my thoughts. *I'll deal with the visions later*, I told myself. It didn't help to overthink everything right now. There were too many questions and not enough answers. Maybe it was time to dig deeper, to confront the memories I had been suppressing for so long.

But for now, I focused on the task at hand. I picked up my phone, opened the food delivery app, and started browsing the menu. I could feel the weight of the visions lingering in the back of my mind, but I tried to push them aside, if only for a little while. There was no point in trying to unravel everything all at once. Though deep down, I knew that sooner or later, I would have to face the truth—whatever it was. The visions weren't going away. They were only getting stronger, and I needed to figure out why. With these thoughts in my head, I placed the order for biryani.

My mom said, "Sweetie, there is a file on the top shelf in my room. Can you get it for me?"

I replied, "Sure, Mom, I'll get it for you."

I walked up the flight of stairs, my head distracted by the swirl of thoughts running through it. Each step felt heavier than the last, and I couldn't shake the feeling that something was on the edge of my mind, something I couldn't quite grasp. The familiar sound of my feet tapping against the stairs was drowned out by the buzz of my thoughts.

As I reached the top, my mom's voice floated up from downstairs, clear but distant. "You'll find the file to the right when you open the doors of the top shelf."

I made it to the last step, stepping onto the floor in complete silence. The stillness of the house contrasted sharply with the chaos of my mind, where thoughts and questions continued to race around. It was as though everything in the house was still, but my brain was spinning.

I made my way into my mother's room. The quietness felt louder here, and the air smelled of something familiar—maybe lavender or dust. But it didn't matter. I focused on the top shelf, knowing the file she needed was there. The wooden doors of the shelf creaked open, and just as I reached for the file, a book fell from its place, hitting the floor with a soft thud that shattered the silence.

I paused, frowning, and bent down to pick up the book. As I lifted it, a photo slipped out from between its pages, fluttering to the ground. I leaned down to grab the photo and glanced at it.

It was a picture of my mother and father, smiling together on a bike. I had seen that bike before. In fact, I'd been trying to remember where I had seen it. The realization hit me like a sudden jolt. This was the same bike from my visions—it was my father's bike, one we had worked on together. The same bike I had seen in my vision right before I was about to go on a road trip, a trip I had no memory of but now realized was part of my past.

It was like a veil lifting. Those fragmented, almost dreamlike flashes I had been having weren't random after all. They were memories—real moments from my life that I had somehow forgotten. This bike, the road trip, my father—everything was starting to come together.

I stared at the photo, feeling a strange mix of clarity and confusion. I placed the book back on the shelf, carefully sliding the photo back into its pages before grabbing the file my mom had asked for. I took a deep breath, holding the file in my hands like it was something more than just paper.

I made my way back downstairs, my legs moving almost automatically. I handed the file to my mom, who glanced at me with a playful smile. "Took you long enough," she teased, her tone light.

I opened my mouth to reply but couldn't find the words. I wasn't sure what to say, what to think, or even how to process the flood of memories rushing through me. Instead, I quietly walked over to the couch and sat down, my hands gripping the edge of the cushion as I tried to ground myself. I felt like I had uncovered something important, something profound, but it was still too fresh, too overwhelming to fully understand.

I sat there, lost in thought, the weight of the photo and the bike and the visions all hanging heavily in the air. I didn't know what it all meant yet, but I had a feeling my life was about to take a turn, one I wasn't prepared for but had been unknowingly waiting for.

CHAPTER 8

SHRUTHI

One month later:

I sat down in my usual spot in class, my eyes automatically scanning the room as I absentmindedly pulled out my notebook. The rhythmic sound of my pen clicking in and out echoed in the otherwise quiet classroom. The familiar chatter of my classmates filled the space, but my thoughts were elsewhere. It had been on my mind all morning, and now, as the moment approached, my heart raced with anticipation.

Mahesh, my best friend, walked in, his loud voice cutting through the air like it always did. His mischievous grin was unmistakable as he headed straight toward me. I couldn't help but notice the playful gleam in his eyes. He knew something was up.

"So, today is finally the day, huh? The day you'll be telling Ronnie about how you feel," Mahesh said with a teasing tone as he plopped down beside me.

I took a deep breath and gave him a small, nervous smile. "Yes, today is the day. I've been thinking about it for a while now. I'm planning to ask him if he wants to go for a walk in the campus during the break. Hopefully, you guys won't tag along this time."

Mahesh laughed, shaking his head. "Don't worry, I won't be crashing your little moment. It's all yours. You can have as much privacy as you need."

I felt a rush of nerves mixed with excitement. Mahesh was right about one thing—this was *my* moment, and I had to make it count. As if on cue, I noticed Ronnie walking into the classroom, his presence like a magnet drawing my gaze.

"Quiet down, Mahesh. Ronnie's here," I muttered under my breath, trying to calm the nerves in my stomach.

"Hey, Ronnie, nice shirt! You're looking good today," I said, with a smile as I made eye contact with him. He returned my smile and casually brushed a hand through his hair.

"Thanks, Shruthi," he replied, his voice warm. I could hear the hint of a smile in it, and my heart skipped a beat. I quickly turned my attention to the professor as he entered the room.

The class began, but my mind wandered, hardly able to focus on the lecture. I kept sneaking glances at Ronnie, my thoughts consumed with the idea of finally telling him how I felt. Each glance made my heart beat a little faster, and I couldn't help but wonder how he might react. Would he laugh? Would he reject me? Or would he say yes? There was only one way to find out.

Before I knew it, the class was over. The bell rang, signaling the start of our break. My heart was thudding in my chest, and I could feel the butterflies fluttering wildly in my stomach. I waited for the perfect moment, and as I watched Ronnie gather his things, I couldn't help but feel the weight of the situation bearing down on me. This was it—the moment I had been waiting for.

"Hey, Ronnie," I called out as casually as I could, my voice slightly trembling. "Do you want to take a walk around the college? I've been meaning to talk to you about something."

He looked up at me, his eyes meeting mine, and a smile formed on his lips. "Sure. A walk sounds good."

I felt a wave of relief wash over me, but the nervousness quickly crept back in. Mahesh, as promised, had already taken Ram and Karan to the canteen, so it was just me and Ronnie. We began walking side by side, the silence between us comfortable yet thick with unspoken tension. My mind raced as the words I had rehearsed countless times echoed in my head.

As we walked down the path, the cool breeze brushing against my face did little to calm the storm of emotions inside me. I could feel my heart pounding in my chest as I took a deep breath, gathering the courage I needed to say the words.

"Ronnie, there's something I've been meaning to tell you," I started, my voice quieter than usual. "I really like you. A lot. Ever since the first time I saw you in class, when you were looking out the window, I was looking at you, couldn't stop thinking about you. And I've been trying to figure out how to say this, but here it goes... will you be my boyfriend?"

The words rushed out in a single breath, and I felt my cheeks turn bright red with embarrassment. My heart was pounding so loudly that I thought for sure he could hear it. I waited for his response, anxiety bubbling up inside me as I glanced at him, hoping I hadn't just made the biggest mistake of my life.

Ronnie stopped walking for a moment, looking at me with a soft smile on his face. I felt the air around us still, almost like time had paused for just a second. His eyes locked onto mine, and for a moment, all I could hear was the rapid beat of my heart.

"Yes," he said, his voice gentle but filled with sincerity. "I would love to be your boyfriend."

The relief I felt in that instant was overwhelming. All the nervousness, all the fear, all the uncertainty evaporated in a rush. I couldn't contain the grin that spread across my face. My heart soared, and I felt lighter than I had in days. The world suddenly seemed brighter, and all the anxiety that had been knotted in my chest was replaced with pure happiness.

"Really?" I asked, my voice barely above a whisper, still trying to process what had just happened.

Ronnie nodded, his smile matching mine. "Yes, really."

We continued walking, and I felt as though I was almost floating. The rest of the break passed in a blur as I tried to get used to the idea that I was now dating Ronnie. The thought of him holding my hand, of being with him, felt surreal in the best possible way. We chatted casually as we walked, but most of my attention was focused on the fact that he was now my boyfriend.

As we reentered the classroom, Mahesh looked up at me, his eyes narrowing slightly as he studied my face. It didn't take him long to figure it out.

"By the look on your face, I don't even need to ask how it went," Mahesh said, grinning from ear to ear. "It looks like it went really well."

I blushed, my face lighting up with a smile. "I still can't believe it. He said yes. Ronnie actually said yes!"

The rest of the day passed in a haze. Every time I looked at Ronnie, my heart skipped a beat. It felt like I was walking on air, and nothing could bring me down from the high I was on.

Later that evening, after the sun had dipped below the horizon and the sky had turned a soft shade of purple, Ronnie invited me to a café. We walked there together, and as we entered the warm, cozy space, I couldn't help but smile at the peaceful atmosphere. The place was both comfortable and intimate, making it the perfect spot for a date.

"The ambiance of this place is nice," Ronnie commented, looking around with a relaxed smile. "I've heard their pizzas are really good."

We settled into a booth, and Ronnie quickly ordered a couple of pizzas for us to share. The food arrived promptly, and I took a bite, savoring the flavor. But if I'm being honest, I hardly noticed the pizza. My attention was entirely on Ronnie—my boyfriend. The way he smiled, the way he looked at me, it was all so perfect that I could hardly believe it was real.

As I reached for my water glass, my fingers brushed against it, and the glass tipped over, spilling water all over

Ronnie's lap. My heart skipped a beat as I quickly stood up, my face flushing with embarrassment.

"Oh no, I'm so sorry!" I stammered, frantic. "I didn't mean to spill water on you. I swear, I wasn't paying attention. Are you okay?"

Ronnie looked at me, his expression unfazed, and to my relief, he broke into a chuckle. "It's fine, Shruthi. Don't worry about it."

Still, I couldn't help but feel guilty. "I feel like I ruined our date," I said softly, my eyes flickering down to the wet patch on his pants.

Ronnie shook his head, a playful grin spreading across his face. "You didn't ruin anything," he said, and then, to my surprise, he grabbed his own glass of water and deliberately spilled it on his already wet lap. He laughed as he did so, looking at me with a twinkle in his eye, to ease my misery.

The sound of his laughter made me laugh too, and I felt all the tension in my body melt away. The incident, which had initially filled me with worry, turned into one of those moments that would become a fond memory— one I'd look back on and smile about.

The rest of the evening passed by in a blur, with us talking and laughing. The café had a comfortable, low-key vibe, and it felt like the perfect setting for our first date as a couple. I found myself stealing glances at him, and every time our eyes met, it felt like something magical was happening.

As the night came to a close, Ronnie dropped me off at my place. We lingered outside for a few moments, the cool night air brushing against my skin. I felt an overwhelming sense of happiness and contentment, knowing that this moment, this feeling, was something I would cherish forever.

"I had a great time tonight," I said softly, my heart still racing.

"Me too," Ronnie replied, his voice warm. Then, before I could say anything else, he wrapped his arms around me, pulling me into a hug. It was gentle but full of meaning, and for a moment, I felt like I was in heaven.

When the hug broke, I stood there for a moment, smiling shyly at him. "Bye, Ronnie," I said, feeling a blush creeping onto my cheeks.

He smiled back, his eyes soft. "Bye, Shruthi. Take care. I'll see you soon."

He waited until I had safely entered my home before driving off. As I watched him leave, I felt a sense of peace settle over me.

I stepped into the house, my heart still racing from what had just happened. The evening had been perfect—every moment filled with laughter, warmth, and the gentle realization that I was no longer just a friend to Ronnie but something more. I walked into the living room, the familiar smell of home wrapped around me, bringing a sense of comfort after such an exciting day.

The living room lights were on, and I could see my dad sitting at the dining table, finishing up his meal. I paused for a moment, trying to calm the flurry of emotions inside me before I greeted him.

I made my way to the hall and sat down on the couch, still trying to process everything. My dad was always observant, and I knew that he could sense when something was different, when something had changed in me. He finished his meal and cleaned up, moving gracefully toward the hall with the same steady steps he always took. He looked at me with a knowing smile, eyes twinkling with curiosity.

"So," he began, settling himself into the chair across from me, "How was your date with Ronnie?"

I smiled, feeling both excited and a little shy. "The date went well," I replied, my voice betraying a mix of joy and disbelief. It was still surreal to think that it had actually happened—Ronnie and I, together. It felt like a dream, one I didn't want to wake up from.

My dad leaned forward slightly, his smile widening as he playfully raised an eyebrow. "When will I finally meet this special boy of yours? I'm sure he's as wonderful as you say."

I felt my cheeks heat up, a soft blush spreading across my face as I thought about Ronnie. "Pretty soon," I replied, my voice filled with affection, as I imagined the next time I'd see him. My dad had always been a huge support, and I wanted him to know about Ronnie, and understand the way I feel about Ronnie.

He chuckled softly, clearly pleased by the way things were going. "Well, I'm looking forward to meeting him," he said, his tone gentle but filled with warmth. He said, "You deserve someone special, my dear."

I felt a wave of gratitude wash over me. It was moments like these that made me realize how lucky I was to have a dad who supported me unconditionally, who wanted nothing more than for me to be happy.

As much as I wanted to stay and talk more about the date, a wave of exhaustion suddenly swept over me. The day had been full of excitement, and the emotional rollercoaster of finally confessing my feelings to Ronnie had drained me more than I realized. "I'm tired, Dad," I said, standing up from the couch and stretching my arms. "I think I'll go to my room and get some sleep."

He nodded, his smile softening as he glanced at me with a fatherly gaze. "Okay, Shruthi," he said, his voice filled with affection. "Good night. Sleep well."

I smiled back at him, feeling a deep sense of peace. "Good night, Dad," I replied before heading down the hallway to my room.

As I entered my room, I shut the door behind me and walked over to my bed. The coolness of the sheets against my skin felt soothing, and I sank into the softness, letting out a long sigh. I closed my eyes for a moment, still basking in the glow of the day's events. But the moment I laid down, my mind began to race once more. The images of Ronnie kept flashing before my eyes—his smile, the way he had looked at me when I asked him to be my boyfriend, the warmth in his voice when he said yes. Everything about the day felt so surreal, yet so real at the same time.

I closed my eyes once again, and this time, sleep came much easier. My heart was at peace, and with images of Ronnie filling my thoughts, I drifted into a restful slumber.

CHAPTER 9

THE SAME NIGHT

After returning home from the date, I entered to find my mom lounging on the sofa in the living room, engrossed in her book. I quietly settled into a chair nearby. She placed the book down, its cover facing up, the pages still open, and took off her glasses. With a soft smile, she looked at me, her eyes sparkling with curiosity. "How was the date, Ronnie?" she asked.

I leaned back slightly, feeling a warmth in my chest, and replied, "The date went well." She raised an eyebrow, clearly interested, and asked, "When will I be meeting this special girl?" I grinned, feeling a bit playful and said, "Pretty soon, Mom."

There was a brief moment of quiet before I let out a small yawn. "I'm tired. I think I'll go to my room and sleep," I added.

She nodded understandingly, her voice soft with affection. "Okay, Ronnie, good night."

I returned her smile and said, "Good night, Mom."

I made my way to my room, closing the door behind me. As I walked over to the bed, the weight of the day slowly pressed down on me. I lay down on the soft mattress, but just as I closed my eyes to sleep, a sudden vision struck me—uninvited, unexpected, but vivid.

VISION:

I was riding with no destination in mind, no set route to follow, simply letting the road guide me wherever it may lead. The freedom of the open road was intoxicating, the world passing by in a blur of green fields and distant mountains. There was something so liberating about it— the sense of being untethered, unbound by time or place. The only thing that mattered in those moments was the road beneath me and the sound of the wind whistling past my ears.

As I cruised along, my mind wandered, and I got lost in the rhythmic hum of the engine. It wasn't about getting to a specific place; it was about the journey itself, the experience of riding, of feeling alive. But then, a familiar sound cut through my thoughts—the blinking of the fuel indicator. I glanced at it quickly and saw the low fuel light flashing urgently, almost as if it were screaming at me, warning me that I was running on empty.

Sighing, I decided it was time to stop. Not far ahead, I spotted a fuel station perched on the side of the highway, like an oasis in the midst of the vast, open road. I pulled over, slowing my bike to a stop in front of the pump. The fuel attendant, a young man in his twenties, looked up from his seat as I parked. He had a bored expression on his face, as though this was just another monotonous day in his routine of refueling vehicles. But when his eyes caught sight of my full riding gear, they sparkled with a hint of amusement.

"Sir, you're all geared up," he said, leaning against the pump and giving me a curious glance. "Where are you headed?"

I chuckled lightly, taking off my helmet before answering him. "I don't really have a place in mind," I replied, a carefree smile tugging at the corners of my lips. "Just riding wherever the road takes me."

The attendant raised an eyebrow, clearly intrigued. "That sounds amazing," he said, almost wistfully. "I've always wanted to go on a road trip like that, you know, explore new places. But first, I need to save up for my bike."

I smiled at him, his enthusiasm infectious. "Good luck with that," I said, giving him an encouraging nod. "I hope you get to live your dream soon."

As I stood there, listening to the hum of the fuel pump and watching the attendant fill up the tank, I couldn't help but reflect on the moment. Here I was, living out a dream that someone else longed for. It made me realize how lucky I was to be able to do this—to have the freedom to explore, to follow the road without any specific destination. I was truly blessed to have this experience, and I didn't want to take it for granted.

Once the bike was filled up, I thanked the attendant and made my way back onto the road. My stomach had started to rumble, reminding me that I hadn't eaten anything since early morning. I spotted a small restaurant just a few meters ahead of the fuel station, the kind of place that looked simple yet inviting. My mouth watered as I thought of the warm, comforting food that awaited me.

The restaurant had the typical ambiance of a roadside eatery—modest yet cozy, with wooden tables and chairs arranged in neat rows. A few other travelers sat inside, quietly enjoying their meals. I walked up to the counter and ordered the South Indian classic—masala dosa. The thought of crispy dosa with spicy chutney made my stomach growl even louder, and I eagerly found a seat by the window.

It didn't take long for the dosa to arrive, steaming hot and golden brown, and its crisp edges inviting me to dig in. I took my first bite, savoring the blend of flavors—the slight crunch of the dosa, the spice of the chutney, and the softness of the potato filling. It was good, no doubt about that, but not the best I'd ever had. I took another bite, and then another, content with the simple pleasure of a hearty meal after a long ride. It may not have been as good as the dosas I've had before, but it was satisfying enough for now.

Finishing the meal, I paid the bill and left the restaurant, stepping back into the warm, humid air. I put my helmet on, secured it tightly, and swung my leg over the bike. I was ready to hit the road again, to continue the journey that had no end in sight. There was no rush, no deadline to meet—just the open highway ahead, waiting to be explored.

As the kilometers passed by, I lost track of time. The sun hung high in the sky, its rays beating down on the road, making the asphalt shimmer in the heat. I could feel the sweat trickling down my back, the hot air pressing against my skin as I rode. However, despite the relentless weather, I couldn't help but appreciate the serenity of the moment. The world around me was so vast, so open, and I felt like a small part of it all.

I pulled over to the side of the road to take a break, my legs aching from the long ride and the sun beating down on me. I took a long sip from the water bottle I had stashed in my backpack, the cool liquid refreshing me as it washed away the dryness in my throat. There was nothing like the feeling of water quenching your thirst, especially after hours of riding under the harsh sun. I looked around as I sat there, feeling the heat of the day and the peace that surrounded me. I realized I had reached Dindigul, and without thinking, I continued on NH 183.

The road stretched before me, winding and curving as I cruised on, feeling the freedom of the open road. After a few hours, I saw a sign for Munnar. Something about the name caught my attention, and without a second thought, I turned my bike in that direction. It was as if the bike itself was drawn to that path, urging me to follow it. As I rode further, the road began to ascend, the curves growing steeper as I climbed into the Western Ghats.

The cool breeze picked up as I reached higher altitudes, and I felt the air change around me. The landscape transformed into a lush paradise—rolling hills dotted with tea plantations, the green of the fields stretching as far as the eye could see. The clouds hung low in the sky, wrapping the hills in a soft mist, while raindrops lightly kissed my skin. The monsoon season had arrived in full force, and the atmosphere felt magical, as though I had entered another world.

I stopped for a moment to take it all in. The view before me was nothing short of breathtaking. The lush green hills seemed to stretch endlessly, like a painting that had come to life. A rainbow arched across the sky, its colors vibrant against the backdrop of the rainclouds. The air was crisp and fresh, the scent of wet earth and tea leaves mingling in the breeze. I sat there on my bike, completely engrossed in the scene before me, feeling as if I had entered heaven.

It was then that I felt a soft hand on my shoulder. Startled, I turned around and met with the most beautiful sight I had ever seen. A girl stood there, her brown eyes warm and kind, her long silky hair cascading down her back like a waterfall. Her skin was fair and flawless, glowing like the full moon. She looked like an angel, and for a moment, I couldn't believe she was real.

Her lips moved, and I could see her speaking, but I was so mesmerized by her beauty that the words she said didn't register. She tapped me on the shoulder to get my attention, and I snapped back into reality.

"Excuse me," she said, her voice soft but clear. "Could you drop me off at my hotel down the road?"

I blinked, still a little dazed, but nodded. "Yes, of course, I am heading that way," I replied, my voice hoarse from the unexpected encounter.

She smiled, a smile that seemed capable of lighting up a thousand houses, and introduced herself. "I'm Neha," she said, her voice sweet and melodious.

"Hi, Neha," I said, trying to keep my composure. "I'm Ronnie."

She hopped onto my bike, and as I revved the engine, I felt my heart fluttering in my chest. Her breath was warm against my neck as she held on behind me, and I could feel my heart race in response. The ride to her hotel was short, but in those few minutes, I found myself lost in the sensation of having her so close.

As we reached her hotel, she thanked me with another radiant smile, and I felt my heart skip a beat. I watched her walk towards the entrance, and for a moment, I found myself replaying the unexpected encounter. That was when I realized that I didn't have to search for a hotel myself—I could stay at the same hotel as Neha.

I walked into the hotel lobby and looked around, but I couldn't spot her anywhere. I had forgotten to ask for her number, and the thought of maybe seeing her again made me feel happy. I approached the receptionist and asked, "Do you have any rooms available?"

"Yes, sir, we do," the receptionist replied. "It will be three thousand rupees per night, after tax. How many nights will you need?"

"Three nights," I answered quickly, eager to settle in. The thought of staying in the same hotel, even if I didn't see her again, gave me a sense of comfort.

After completing the formalities, the receptionist handed me my room keys. I took the elevator up to my floor, and as I stepped into the room, I was greeted by the sweet fragrance of lavender. The scent was calming, and as I entered the room, I was struck by how peaceful everything seemed. The bed looked inviting, and I couldn't resist. I stretched my arms and legs before lying down, sinking into the softness of the mattress. The exhaustion from the long ride and the events of the day caught up with me, and before I knew it, I was fast asleep, ready to take on whatever tomorrow would bring.

CHAPTER 10

I woke up to the soft warmth of the sun's rays entering through the balcony doors, their golden light gently coaxing me out of sleep like a mother's hand waking her child. The light filled the room, easing away the lingering fog of sleep from my mind. I sat up in bed, stretching, feeling a rush of rejuvenation coursing through me from the long and peaceful night's sleep. There was something deeply satisfying about waking up after a good night's rest, the kind that leaves you feeling refreshed and ready to take on the day ahead.

As I ran a hand through my hair, my phone began to ring. It was a call from my mom. A smile spread across my face as I answered it, my voice bright with warmth.

"Hi, Mom!" I greeted her cheerfully.

Her voice came through the phone, comforting and familiar. "How are you, Ronnie? Did you sleep well?"

"I did, Mom. Slept like a baby," I replied, glancing out the balcony at the picturesque scene before me. The early morning sun filtered through the trees, casting long, dappled shadows across the lush landscape. The tall trees were outlined against the horizon, their leaves swaying gently in the breeze as the clouds drifted lazily above. It was a lovely morning, the kind that filled you with peace and contentment just by witnessing it.

"I'm glad, dear," my mom said, her voice softening with affection. "I just wanted to check in. Take care of yourself, alright?"

"I will, Mom. Don't worry," I said, stepping out onto the balcony. My gaze drifted to the left, and there, standing on the adjacent balcony, was Neha. Her hair was blowing slightly in the wind, and she looked elegant in the early morning light. Her gaze met mine, and she smiled, a playful glint in her eyes.

She jokingly called out, "Hey! Are you following me?"

I couldn't help but laugh at her teasing. "Maybe. After all, seeing your beauty just once wasn't enough for me."

Her cheeks turned a soft shade of pink, her fair skin glowing in the sunlight. The sight of her smiling, her eyes shining with a quiet amusement, filled me with a strange and intoxicating feeling. It was as though time stood still for a moment. I wanted to imprint that image in my mind forever, to carry it with me no matter where life would take me.

I continued, "Now that we've established that I'm following you, how about I follow you around today and explore the place with you?"

Neha's smile widened, and her eyes sparkled with a mix of curiosity and excitement. "I would love that," she said, her voice light and cheerful.

"Great!" I said, feeling a surge of excitement. "I'll meet you in an hour, then. Be ready!"

As soon as she disappeared from view, I jumped up and down like a little kid, my heart racing at the thought of spending the day with her. The whole idea felt surreal, and I quickly grabbed my phone to look up nearby places to visit. My eyes fell upon a name—Attukal Waterfalls. It sounded perfect. I quickly made a mental note to visit it.

I took a shower, letting the warm water wash away any remaining drowsiness—not that there would be any after witnessing the beauty in the adjacent balcony—then began picking out my clothes. After some deliberation, I decided on a classic combination—my favorite round-neck white T-shirt, a denim jacket, and jeans. I stood in front of the mirror, checking my reflection one last time before heading out.

When I opened the door to leave, I found myself standing right in front of Neha's room. Taking a deep breath to calm my nerves, I knocked softly on the door. Just as my hand lifted to knock again, the door swung open, and there she was.

Neha was wearing a black top paired with jeans, and a jacket draped casually over her shoulders. The soft, floral scent of her perfume floated towards me, and I inhaled deeply, momentarily distracted by her presence. She looked effortlessly stunning—so natural, so beautiful. It was as if the world itself paused to witness her grace.

"You look very beautiful," I said, unable to hide the admiration in my voice.

Her lips curled into a playful smile, and she tilted her head slightly. "Was I not looking beautiful before?" she teased, her eyes dancing with laughter.

I laughed along, feeling a warmth spread through me. "You always look beautiful," I said, my voice sincere.

We headed downstairs, stepping out of the hotel into the cool morning air. The streets of Munnar were still calm, the world gently waking up. As we walked toward the bike, the quiet hum of the town greeted us, the soft rustle of leaves in the trees adding to the peaceful ambiance. I started the engine, and she hopped on behind me.

I could hear her stomach rumble, and I turned my head slightly, smiling. "How about breakfast?" I asked. "I think we both could use something to eat."

She laughed softly, a light and melodic sound. "Yeah, I'm starving."

I asked a local for directions to a place that served a good breakfast, and he pointed us down the road. We followed his directions, and soon enough, we found ourselves in front of a small but busy eatery. The crowd inside was a clear sign that the food was good, and I was eager to taste it.

After finishing breakfast and feeling full, we set off again. The road stretched out before us, and I could feel the thrill of the open road as I revved the engine. Munnar's beauty unfolded around us—rolling green hills, misty clouds, and tea plantations that seemed to stretch on forever. The air was fresh, filled with the scent of wet earth and tea leaves, and I couldn't help but glance in the rearview mirror every so often, captivated by the sight of Neha's face reflected in the glass. Her eyes were bright, her expression peaceful, and I couldn't help but feel a deep sense of happiness.

As we rode, her hair flew in the wind majestically, and I found myself momentarily distracted by how perfect everything felt. It was as if the universe had conspired to make this moment just right.

"Where are we going?" Neha asked, breaking my thought.

"It's a surprise," I replied, grinning.

We continued driving through Munnar, the landscape growing even more breathtaking with every passing kilometer. The roads twisted and turned, leading us deeper into the mountains. As we approached the Attukal Waterfalls, we could hear the melodious sound of water rushing over rocks. The sound grew louder as we neared the falls, and when we finally arrived, I was struck with a sense of awe.

The sight before us was nothing short of magical. The milky white water cascaded over large rocks, flowing down into the valley below. The lush greenery surrounding the falls seemed to embrace the water, creating a serene and peaceful atmosphere. The mist from the waterfall rose up in a fine spray, kissing our faces and making everything feel even more surreal.

I looked over at Neha, and my heart skipped a beat. She stood there, lost in the beauty of nature. A few pearls of water gathered at the corner of her eyes, and I realized she was moved by the sight. There was something so pure and beautiful about the way she looked at that moment. She was happy, her smile radiating a quiet joy that made my heart swell.

She turned to me, her face glowing with happiness, and said, "Thank you for bringing me here."

Her words made me smile, and without thinking, I leaned in and kissed her. Her soft lips met mine, and in that moment, everything else seemed to fade away. The rush of emotions that flooded through me was overwhelming—warmth, happiness, contentment. When we pulled away, her face was flushed with a mix of shyness and innocence, and I couldn't help but smile.

We walked back to the bike in silence, the weight of the moment still hanging between us. I revved the engine, and we started heading back to the hotel. As I rode, the wind in my face and the tingling sensation from the kiss still fresh on my lips, I couldn't help but feel that everything about the moment was perfect.

But that fleeting perfection was shattered in an instant, because in the next moment, as we approached a curve on the road, something went wrong. The rear tire of the bike slipped, and before I could react, I felt myself being thrown off. The world spun, and everything went black.

PRESENT

I jolted out from my sleep, and saw that the sun was out. My heart raced as I tried to make sense of my vision. The events from my vision—Neha, the waterfall, the kiss— flashed before my eyes. But something didn't feel right.

Frantically, I searched for my mother. I needed answers. I spotted her sitting on the sofa in the living room.

I scrambled to sit up, my heart pounding in my chest. "Mom, what happened to the girl? The one who was with me during the accident?" I asked, my voice shaking.

My mother looked at me, confusion clouding her features. "What girl, Ronnie?" she replied gently. "There was no girl with you. You were the only one at the accident scene, and only you were taken to the hospital. There was no one else admitted along with you."

Her words hit me like a ton of bricks. The visions I had experienced—the ones with Neha—were all memories from my past before the accident. But according to my mother, there had been no girl with me at the time of the accident. No Neha.

I was left with a question that gnawed at me: If the visions were true, then what had happened to her? Where is she?

CHAPTER 11

3 WEEKS LATER

It was a typical evening when I met Shruthi at our usual hangout spot, a cozy little café tucked away on a quiet street. We had frequented this place often, drawn to its warm lights and soft music that always created the perfect atmosphere. It was the kind of place where time seemed to slow down, allowing you to just be, to relax, to enjoy the moment.

Shruthi was already there when I arrived, sitting at a booth that had become her regular spot over the past few weeks. Her eyes lit up when she saw me, and she waved me over with a bright smile. I smiled back, but something felt different this time. My heart wasn't racing like it usually did when I saw her. Instead, there was a sense of numbness, a distance that I couldn't explain, but which I knew had been growing inside me for some time now.

I walked over to the booth and sat down across from her. She handed me one of her earbuds, and I put it in, feeling the soft hum of the music fill my ears. It was a slow and melodic love song, and as the notes played, I couldn't help but notice how beautiful Shruthi looked in that moment. But as much as I wanted to feel something, anything, my mind kept wandering to a different place, a different person.

As the song played on, Shruthi leaned closer to me, her face softening. Before I could stop her, she kissed me. Her lips were warm and gentle against mine, but the sensation was empty. There was no spark, no fire, nothing like what I had felt in my visions. The kiss, which should have been full of emotion, left me cold, and in that moment, the truth hit me like a crashing wave: I had no feelings for Shruthi.

Pulling back gently, I stared into her eyes, unsure of how to explain what was happening inside me. Her smile faded as she searched my face for an answer. I took a deep breath, gathering my thoughts.

"Shruthi, I'm sorry," I began, my voice trembling. "I have no feelings for you. I... I'm in love with someone else. Someone I met before college started. A girl I've been seeing in my visions."

Her eyes widened with surprise, confusion, and hurt. "What do you mean, Ronnie? We've been seeing each other for a few weeks, and you're telling me this *now*? Just like that?"

"I never wanted to hurt you," I said quietly, feeling the weight of the words. "But the truth is, I've been thinking about someone else. Someone I met on a trip. I can't get her out of my mind."

The silence between us was heavy, suffocating. Shruthi nodded, her face a mixture of disappointment and sadness. She didn't say anything, just looked down at her hands, trying to process what I had just told her. I couldn't bear to stay any longer, not like this. I stood up abruptly, my chair scraping against the floor.

"I'm sorry, Shruthi," I whispered, the words sounding hollow to my ears as I turned and left the café.

I walked out into the night, feeling a strange emptiness wash over me. It wasn't the kind of emptiness I'd felt before, when I was alone. No, this was different. It was the kind of emptiness that comes from realizing you've lost something important. My feelings for Shruthi were real, I had cared about her once, but now that I knew who I truly loved, there was no going back. And I couldn't explain it. I didn't even fully understand it myself.

When I arrived home, I found my mother sitting in the hall, as usual, her nose buried in a book. She looked up when I entered, her face softening in a knowing smile. But that smile faded when she saw the tears in my eyes.

"Ronnie, what's wrong?" she asked, her voice filled with concern.

I sank down onto the couch beside her, feeling the weight of the world on my shoulders. I didn't know where to begin. How could I explain this strange series of visions, this love that had come from nowhere and seemed to consume me entirely?

I wiped my eyes with the back of my hand and took a deep breath. "Mom, I've been having these visions. They're not dreams, they're... memories. I met a girl on the trip, and I fell in love with her. I don't know what happened to her, but I need to find her. I can't stop thinking about her."

My mom placed her book down and gently took my hands in hers, her touch warm and reassuring. "Ronnie, it sounds like you love this girl deeply. And if that's how you feel, then you have to go find her. Don't stop until you do. You deserve to know the truth, to know what happened to her."

Her words were simple, but they hit me with the force of a revelation. Maybe it was time to stop pretending, to stop fighting the feelings I had been suppressing. If I truly loved her, then I couldn't let anything stand in my way.

I stood up abruptly, my mind made up. "I'm going. I'm going to Munnar. I'll find her."

My mom looked at me, her expression soft with understanding. "Be careful, Ronnie. And remember, sometimes the answers you're looking for aren't what you expect."

I packed a small bag, throwing a few clothes into it before grabbing my keys. My heart pounded in my chest as I hopped on my bike and revved the engine. The road ahead was uncertain, but I felt an overwhelming sense of urgency, like I was chasing something that could slip through my fingers at any moment.

The wind whipped through my hair as I sped toward Munnar, the memories of my visions still vivid in my mind. I had to find her. I couldn't explain why, but I knew that I had to.

Arriving in Munnar, the familiar sights from my vision overwhelmed me. The streets, the shops, the people—they all felt like pieces of a puzzle finally coming together. I retraced my steps, going to the hotel where I had dropped Neha off. It looked exactly the same, just like I remembered.

I approached the front desk, hoping for some answers. "Excuse me," I said to the receptionist, trying to keep my voice steady. "I'm looking for a girl who stayed here a while ago. Her name is Neha."

The receptionist looked at me, his face expressionless. "I'm sorry, sir. No one by that name has stayed here for the time period you mentioned."

The words hit me like a slap in the face. I had followed every detail from my vision, and yet, here I was, standing in front of someone who seemed to have no knowledge of the girl I was desperately searching for. I pressed on with a few more questions, but didn't get the answers I was hoping for. Everything was falling apart. My heart sank, and the weight of uncertainty settled over me. Everything I had seen in my visions—the hotel, the streets, the waterfall—was real. She also must be real.

Five days passed, and despite my best efforts, I couldn't find her. I had visited every place I had seen in my visions, searched every corner of Munnar, and yet there was no sign of Neha. It was like she had vanished into thin air. My frustration and hopelessness grew with each passing day, but something inside me refused to give up. I couldn't stop searching. I couldn't let go of her.

One evening, I returned to the place where I had first seen her. I sat on my bike, my eyes scanning the street, hoping for a glimpse of her. My mind swirled with confusion and nothing seemed to make sense. The sound of the wind in the trees, the hum of passing cars—it all felt distant. Then, out of the corner of my eye, I caught a glimpse of something. A soft, glowing light down the road, shimmering like a beacon.

I looked closer, and there she was. Neha.

It was her. She was standing in front of me, just like in my visions. The same graceful figure, the same elegant beauty, and yet, there was something different this time. The glow surrounding her was almost otherworldly, as if she didn't belong to this world at all. I could feel my heart race, tears welling up in my eyes.

"Neha," I whispered, almost afraid to speak her name out loud. "I've been searching for you for five days. Seeing you again… I don't know how to explain it. I'm so happy. I love you."

Her face seemed to fall. The light in her eyes dimmed, and her expression turned sorrowful.

"We can't be together," she said, her voice soft, almost a whisper. "You have to forget about me."

"Why?" I asked, my heart pounding in my chest. "Why can't we be together?"

Tears welled up in her eyes as she looked at me, the sorrow evident in her face. "I'm not alive, Ronnie. I am just a soul, and I cannot be with you. I never could have been."

The words struck me like a bolt of lightning. My body went cold, my breath caught in my throat. She is… she is a soul? The realization hit me hard, and the world around me seemed to blur.

"Forget about me," she said, tears dripping from her eyes, as she vanished from my sight into thin air.

"*Recognizing that there are both good and bad endings helps us truly move forward.*"

EPILOGUE

SIX YEARS LATER

The evening had descended slowly, the sun dipping low on the horizon. It was that quiet time of day when the world seemed to pause for a moment, suspended between the light of day and the cool embrace of night. I was sitting in a café, holding a cup of freshly brewed coffee in my hands, the steam rising lazily from the mug as I savored the rich, inviting scent of the dark roast. My attention was split between my laptop and the world around me. The soft hum of conversation filled the air, blending with the background clinking of cups and the gentle hiss of the espresso machine.

It was one of those moments when everything seemed to be in perfect harmony. The café was warm, its lighting soft and inviting, and the murmur of voices created a comfortable ambiance. I had become so absorbed in my work that I had almost forgotten where I was—until I felt a subtle shift in the air around me. Without realizing it, I lifted my eyes from the screen and let my gaze wander.

And that's when I saw her.

She was walking toward the café, her figure framed against the fading evening light. The wind caught her hair, sending it swirling around her face, and in that moment, she appeared almost otherworldly. The soft breeze seemed to lift her into a graceful motion, and for a second, she looked like she was gliding rather than walking. She moved with a certain elegance, a quiet confidence that drew my attention, and I found myself momentarily captivated by her presence.

She approached the door to the café, stepping inside with a quiet grace. The sound of the door's chime barely registered in my ears as my eyes followed her movement. She was in her early twenties, dressed in a simple yet elegant outfit—a soft sweater and a pair of jeans. But it wasn't just her clothing that caught my eye. It was the way she carried herself, with an effortless elegance that made her seem both beautiful and untouchable.

For a brief moment, I lost track of time, simply watching as she went to the counter to place her order. She spoke briefly to the barista, her voice soft but clear, before moving toward the cluster of tables scattered across the café. At that moment, my focus returned to my laptop, but even as I resumed typing, there was a part of me that couldn't help but remain aware of her presence, as if she had imprinted herself on my thoughts.

Minutes slipped by, and I became so absorbed in my work that I barely noticed when the café grew slightly quieter. Then, just as I was about to take another sip of my coffee, I heard a soft voice from across the table, pulling me out of my thoughts.

"Hi," the voice said, gentle but not shy. "Can I sit at your table? All the other tables are full."

I froze for a second, unsure if I heard correctly. My eyes flicked up from the screen, and I saw her standing there, looking at me with a soft smile on her face. There was a brief pause as I struggled to process the situation—she was asking to sit with me? My heart skipped a beat, and I felt a rush of surprise flood through me. I hadn't expected her to approach me.

It took a few moments for me to find my voice, to gather my scattered thoughts. The words didn't come immediately, and for a brief second, I felt disoriented by the sheer unexpectedness of it all. But then, realizing I was staring at her without saying anything, I quickly replied, "Oh, uh, yes, of course. You can sit here."

She smiled again, and my heart did a little flip at the warmth in her expression. As she settled into the chair across from me, I tried to calm my racing thoughts. I didn't know why I was so flustered—I had no reason to be. After all, we were strangers to each other. But there was something about her that made me feel nervous, as if meeting her was somehow a momentous occasion.

I returned to my laptop, attempting to resume my work, but I couldn't quite focus. I kept sneaking glances at her, trying not to be obvious. She was pulling out a book from her bag, and as she opened it, I couldn't help but notice that it was a book I had read before. My curiosity aroused, I couldn't help myself.

"That's a lovely book," I said, my voice quieter than I intended, but genuine.

She looked up at me, surprised for a moment, but then her face broke into a knowing smile. "I know, right? It's actually my third time reading it," she said, her voice soft and full of warmth. There was something about the way she spoke—thoughtful, like she genuinely cared about the stories she read. I found myself intrigued and wanting to know more.

"I totally get it," I replied. "I loved it the first time I read it. It's one of those stories that stays with you long after you finish it."

She nodded, her eyes lighting up as she glanced down at the pages. "Exactly. It's like every time I read it, I discover something new."

I smiled, feeling a sudden sense of connection. "It's rare to find a book that does that, isn't it? Most of the time, once you finish, you're done with it. But some books just... keep calling you back."

She laughed softly, the sound floating like a melody in the air. "You're right. It's like the book has a life of its own, and every time I pick it up again, it feels like a new experience."

I was still struck by how easy it was to talk to her. The conversation flowed so naturally, as if we had known each other for much longer than just a few minutes. There was no awkwardness, no hesitation—just a genuine exchange of thoughts and ideas.

By this point, I realized that I should probably introduce myself, since we were talking so comfortably. "By the way," I said, "I'm Ronnie. And you are?"

She looked at me with a warm, genuine smile. "Hi Ronnie, I'm Maya."

It was a simple exchange, but somehow it felt significant, like we had just crossed some invisible threshold and were now on equal footing. We continued to talk about the book, analyzing the characters and the plot, exchanging our thoughts on what made it so special. We laughed over some of the more ridiculous moments and reflected on the deeper themes that the author had explored. As we spoke, I realized that our tastes overlapped in so many areas, but there were also subtle differences that made our conversation even more interesting.

We discussed other books we had read, our favorite genres, and the kind of stories that had left a lasting impact on us. We also found that we had some common hobbies—both of us loved going on road trips, and we shared an interest in food. There were little sparks of excitement every time we discovered something else we had in common. It was easy to talk to her, and every time I looked at her, I found myself captivated by her beauty. Her smile, in particular, was something that stuck with me—bright and genuine, with an effortless warmth that made everything around her feel just a little bit lighter.

Somewhere in the midst of our conversation, I found myself paying her compliments. "You know, Maya, you have the most incredible smile. It's contagious. I don't think I've stopped smiling since you sat down."

She blushed slightly, a soft pink color creeping across her cheeks, but she didn't appear uncomfortable. Instead, she gave me a playful grin. "You're flattering me, Ronnie. But I'll take it."

We laughed, and for a moment, the world outside the café seemed to disappear. Time felt irrelevant as we continued to chat. We weren't in a rush, and it felt like we could talk for hours without running out of things to say. There was a sense of ease between us, a natural rhythm that made everything feel just... right.

Eventually, the conversation slowed as the café began to empty out, signaling that it was time for both of us to leave. We had talked for what felt like an eternity, but the evening was drawing to a close. I gathered my things, not wanting the moment to end, but also not wanting to be the one to make it awkward.

As I stood up, I hesitated for a moment, unsure if it was too soon to ask. But then, I took a deep breath and spoke.

"Maya," I said, my voice a little more tentative than usual, "would you... would you like to go out on a date sometime?"

Her eyes widened for just a split second, and then she smiled—a smile that was both shy and delighted. "Yes," she said softly, "I'd love that, Ronnie."

I felt my heart skip a beat, a surge of joy flooding through me. Her words were like a weight lifting off my chest. I had been nervous, unsure of how she would respond, but now there was nothing but excitement and anticipation. We exchanged phone numbers

As she gathered her things, she turned to me with one last smile. "I'll see you soon, then," she said, her voice warm. "Goodbye for now, Ronnie."

With that, she left, and I watched her walk out of the café, a smile still lingering on my face. I was filled with a sense of hope, knowing that this was only the beginning of something special.